Table Of Contents

Introduction

Importance of marketing in mobile game development

Marketing plays a crucial role in the success of any mobile game. In today's highly competitive mobile gaming industry, it's not enough to simply develop a high-quality game. You need to have a solid marketing strategy to ensure that your game reaches its intended audience and generates the desired revenue.

One of the most important aspects of marketing in mobile game development is understanding your target audience. You need to know who your game is designed for and what their preferences are. This information will help you tailor your marketing efforts to reach the right people with the right message.

Another key part of marketing your mobile game is creating a strong brand identity. This includes everything from your game's name and logo to the design of your website and social media channels. A strong brand identity will help you stand out in a crowded market and make it easier for people to recognize and remember your game.

Social media is also a powerful marketing tool for mobile game developers. Platforms like Facebook, Twitter, and Instagram provide an easy way to reach a large audience and engage with your players. By creating compelling content and interacting with your followers, you can build a strong community around your game and increase its visibility.

Paid advertising is another effective marketing strategy for mobile games. Platforms like Google Ads and Facebook Ads allow you to target specific audiences and track your advertising spend to ensure maximum return on investment. However, it's important to carefully monitor your advertising campaigns to ensure that you're getting the results you want.

In conclusion, marketing is an integral part of mobile game development. By understanding your target audience, creating a strong brand identity, leveraging social media, and using paid advertising, you can increase the visibility of your game and drive revenue. By implementing these strategies, you can ensure that your mobile game stands out in a crowded market and reaches its full potential.

Overview of the book

The mobile gaming industry is rapidly expanding, and the competition is getting more fierce by the day. As a mobile game maker, you need to stay ahead of the competition and develop a marketing strategy that will help you launch your game successfully. This book, "Marketing Your Way to the Top: Proven Mobile Game Launch Strategies," is designed to help you do just that.

This book is a comprehensive guide that covers every aspect of mobile game marketing, from pre-launch planning to post-launch analysis. It is written specifically for mobile game makers who are looking for practical, actionable advice on how to market their games successfully.

The book begins with an overview of the mobile gaming industry and the current state of the market. It then delves into the various marketing channels that are available to mobile game makers, including social media, app store optimization, influencer marketing, and more. Each chapter covers a specific marketing strategy in detail, providing you with step-by-step instructions on how to implement it effectively.

One of the unique features of this book is the case studies included throughout. These case studies highlight real-world examples of mobile game makers who have successfully launched their games using the strategies outlined in the book. By studying these examples, you can gain valuable insights into what works and what doesn't in the world of mobile game marketing.

Finally, the book concludes with a section on post-launch analysis. This section is crucial because it helps you evaluate the success of your marketing efforts and identify areas for improvement. By analyzing your results, you can refine your marketing strategy and make it even more effective for future game launches.

In summary, "Marketing Your Way to the Top: Proven Mobile Game Launch Strategies" is an essential resource for any mobile game maker looking to succeed in this competitive industry. Whether you're a seasoned developer or just starting out, this book has something valuable to offer. So, pick up a copy today and start marketing your way to the top!

Target audience

Target Audience

Before launching a mobile game, it is important to identify your target audience. Your target audience is the group of people who are most likely to be interested in your game and who will ultimately become your customers. Understanding your target audience is crucial to the success of your game launch and marketing strategies.

To identify your target audience, start by considering the genre and theme of your game. For example, if you have developed a puzzle game, your target audience is likely to be people who enjoy challenging games that require problem-solving skills. On the other hand, if you have developed a racing game, your target audience is likely to be people who enjoy fast-paced action and competition.

Once you have identified the genre and theme of your game, you can use market research to further narrow down your target audience. Look at demographic factors such as age, gender, income, and education level. You can also consider psychographic factors such as interests, hobbies, and lifestyles.

Once you have identified your target audience, you can tailor your game launch and marketing strategies to appeal to their interests and preferences. For example, if your target audience is primarily composed of teenagers, you might focus on social media marketing and influencer partnerships to reach them. On the other hand, if your target audience is primarily composed of busy professionals, you might focus on email marketing and mobile app advertising to reach them on-the-go.

In summary, identifying your target audience is a crucial step in the game launch and marketing process. By understanding the interests and preferences of your target audience, you can develop strategies that are specifically tailored to appeal to them. This will increase the chances of your game being successful and reaching its full potential.

Understanding the Mobile Game Market

Market research and analysis

Market research and analysis is a crucial step in any mobile game launch and marketing strategy. It involves gathering and analyzing data about the target audience, competitors, and market trends to make informed decisions about how to position and promote your game.

The first step in market research is to identify your target audience. This includes analyzing demographic data such as age, gender, location, and interests. Understanding your audience will help you tailor your game and marketing efforts to appeal to them.

Competitive analysis is another important aspect of market research. It involves analyzing your competitors' games, their marketing strategies, and their strengths and weaknesses. This information will help you differentiate your game and identify opportunities for improvement.

Market trends analysis involves keeping track of changes and developments in the mobile gaming industry. This includes new technologies, popular game genres, and emerging markets. Staying up-to-date with market trends can give you a competitive edge and help you make informed decisions about your game and marketing strategy.

Once you have gathered and analyzed this data, you can use it to develop a marketing strategy that will effectively reach your target audience and differentiate your game from the competition. This may include tactics such as social media advertising, influencer marketing, app store optimization, and targeted email campaigns.

In conclusion, market research and analysis is a critical step in developing a successful mobile game launch and marketing strategy. By gathering and analyzing data about your audience, competitors, and market trends, you can make informed decisions about how to position and promote your game to achieve maximum success.

Identifying target audience

Identifying target audience is a crucial step in any marketing strategy, and mobile game makers are no exception. Knowing your target audience will help you tailor your game and your marketing efforts to their preferences and needs, maximizing your chances of success.

To identify your target audience, start by analyzing your game's genre, theme, mechanics, and art style. Who would be interested in playing this game? What age range, gender, location, and interests do they have? You can gather this information from market research, surveys, focus groups, social media analytics, and app store reviews of similar games.

Once you have a clear idea of your target audience, you can segment it into different groups based on their behavior, preferences, and demographics. For example, you may have casual players who only play for short periods of time, hardcore players who invest a lot of time and money in the game, or social players who enjoy playing with friends and sharing their achievements on social media. Each group may require a different approach in terms of game design, monetization, and marketing.

Another important aspect of identifying your target audience is understanding their pain points and motivations. Why do they play mobile games? Is it for entertainment, relaxation, competition, social interaction, or learning? What challenges do they face in their daily lives that your game can address or alleviate? By tapping into these emotional triggers, you can create a more engaging and meaningful experience for your players, and increase their loyalty and advocacy.

Finally, it's important to constantly monitor and adapt your target audience as your game evolves and the market changes. Don't assume that your initial assumptions are correct or that your audience will stay the same over time. Use data analytics, player feedback, and industry trends to refine your target audience and adjust your strategy accordingly.

In conclusion, identifying your target audience is a fundamental step in marketing your mobile game. By knowing who your players are, what they want, and how they behave, you can create a game that resonates with them and a marketing campaign that reaches them effectively.

Competitive analysis

Competitive Analysis

One of the most crucial things to do before launching a mobile game is to conduct a competitive analysis. Knowing your competition and understanding their strengths and weaknesses can help you position your game in the market and make informed decisions about your marketing and launch strategies.

Start by identifying your direct competitors – those who make games in the same genre or category as yours. Analyze their games and see what features, mechanics, and user experiences they offer. Take note of their pricing, marketing messages, and user reviews. Look at their social media presence, website, and advertising campaigns.

Next, evaluate their strengths and weaknesses. What makes their games stand out? What are their unique selling points? Are there any areas where they fall short? What do users complain about in their reviews? Answering these questions can help you identify opportunities to differentiate your game and create a unique value proposition.

You should also analyze their marketing and launch strategies. How do they promote their games? Which channels do they use? Do they offer any discounts or promotions? When did they launch their games, and how successful were their launches? Answering these questions can help you identify gaps in the market and create better marketing and launch strategies.

Finally, use the insights you've gathered to refine your game and marketing strategies. Identify areas where you can improve your game's mechanics, features, or user experience. Create a unique value proposition that differentiates your game from the competition. Develop a marketing plan that leverages the strengths of your game and targets the right audience.

Remember, a competitive analysis is an ongoing process. Keep monitoring your competition and the market to stay ahead of the curve and adjust your strategies as needed. By conducting a thorough competitive analysis, you can increase your chances of success and make your mobile game stand out in a crowded market.

Pre-Launch Strategies

Building hype through social media

Building Hype Through Social Media

In today's digitally-driven world, social media has become an essential tool for building hype and creating buzz around new products, including mobile games. With millions of users spanning various platforms like Facebook, Twitter, Instagram, and Snapchat, social media is an effective way to reach a wider audience and generate excitement for your game launch.

Here are some tips for building hype through social media:

1. Create a social media strategy

Before launching your game, it's essential to create a social media strategy that outlines your goals, target audience, content, and posting schedule. This plan should also include a list of influencers and gaming communities that you will reach out to for support.

2. Build anticipation

To generate hype, create teaser content that showcases your game's features, gameplay, and storyline. Use hashtags, countdowns, and sneak peeks to create a sense of anticipation and excitement.

3. Leverage influencers

Influencer marketing is a powerful tool for building hype around your game. Identify influencers that cater to your target audience and collaborate with them to create sponsored content, giveaways, and reviews.

4. Encourage user-generated content

Encourage users to create content related to your game by running contests, challenges, and giveaways. This will not only generate buzz but also foster a sense of community around your game.

5. Engage with your audience

Engage with your audience by responding to comments, messages, and reviews. This will not only build trust but also create a loyal fan base that will help promote your game.

6. Utilize paid advertising

Paid advertising on social media platforms can help you reach a wider audience and generate more buzz. Consider running ads on platforms like Facebook, Instagram, and Twitter to promote your game launch.

In conclusion, building hype through social media is an effective marketing strategy for mobile game makers. By creating a social media strategy, building anticipation, leveraging influencers, encouraging user-generated content, engaging with your audience, and utilizing paid advertising, you can generate excitement and buzz around your game launch.

Creating a strong brand identity

Creating a strong brand identity is essential to the success of any mobile game launch. It helps establish your game in the minds of players and sets it apart from the competition. A strong brand identity also serves as a foundation for all of your marketing efforts, giving you a consistent message to communicate across all channels.

To create a strong brand identity, you need to start by understanding your game's core values and unique selling points. What makes your game special? What sets it apart from other games in the same genre? Once you have a clear understanding of these factors, you can begin developing a visual identity that communicates them effectively.

Your visual identity should include things like a logo, color scheme, and typography. These elements should be consistent across all of your marketing materials, from your website to your social media profiles to your app store listing. They should also be designed to appeal to your target audience and reflect the tone and style of your game.

In addition to your visual identity, you should also develop a brand voice that reflects your game's personality and values. This voice should be used consistently across all of your marketing channels, from your website copy to your social media posts to your in-game messaging. It should be engaging, authentic, and memorable, helping to build a strong emotional connection with your audience.

Finally, you should create a brand style guide that outlines all of your brand identity elements and provides guidelines for their use. This guide should include things like your logo's size and placement, your color palette, and your preferred font choices. By following these guidelines consistently, you can ensure that your brand remains cohesive and recognizable across all channels.

In conclusion, creating a strong brand identity is essential to the success of any mobile game launch. By developing a clear visual identity, brand voice, and style guide, you can establish a strong foundation for all of your marketing efforts and build a strong emotional connection with your audience.

Pre-launch promotions and giveaways

Pre-launch promotions and giveaways are essential tactics for mobile game makers to generate buzz and excitement before the official launch. These strategies can help you build a loyal fan base, increase your social media following, and ultimately drive downloads and revenue.

Here are some effective pre-launch promotions and giveaways you can use to promote your mobile game:

1. Teaser trailers

Creating a teaser trailer for your mobile game is a great way to generate interest and hype. Your trailer should be short and sweet, highlighting the best features of your game and leaving viewers wanting more. Sharing your teaser trailer on social media platforms like YouTube, Instagram, and Facebook can help you reach a wider audience.

2. Social media contests

Contests are a fun way to engage with your audience and promote your mobile game. You can offer prizes like free downloads, in-game currency, or exclusive merchandise to winners. Social media platforms like Twitter, Instagram, and Facebook are great places to run your contests.

3. Influencer partnerships

Partnering with influencers in the gaming community can help you reach a wider audience and build credibility. You can reach out to popular gaming YouTubers, Twitch streamers, and bloggers to promote your game. Offering them early access to your game or exclusive content can help you secure their support.

4. Early access

Giving your loyal fans early access to your game can help generate hype and buzz. You can offer early access to players who sign up for your email list or follow you on social media. This can help you build a loyal fan base before the official launch.

5. Limited-time promotions

Offering limited-time promotions like discounts or special in-game items can help you drive downloads and revenue. You can promote these promotions on social media or through email marketing campaigns.

In conclusion, pre-launch promotions and giveaways are essential tactics for mobile game makers to generate buzz and excitement before the official launch. By using these strategies, you can build a loyal fan base, increase your social media following, and ultimately drive downloads and revenue.

Launch Day

App store optimization

App Store Optimization (ASO) is the process of optimizing mobile apps to rank higher in an app store's search results. The higher your app ranks in the app store, the more visible it will be to potential users, and the more downloads it will receive.

ASO involves optimizing various elements of your app listing, including the title, description, keywords, and visuals. Here are some tips for optimizing these elements:

1. Title: Your app's title should be clear, concise, and memorable. It should also contain relevant keywords that describe what your app does.

2. Description: Your app's description should be informative and persuasive. It should clearly explain what your app does, its features and benefits, and why users should download it. Use relevant keywords in your description to improve your app's search ranking.

3. Keywords: Choose relevant keywords that describe your app's functionality and benefits. Use these keywords in your app's title, description, and tags to improve its visibility in search results.

4. Visuals: Your app's icon and screenshots should be eye-catching and representative of your app's features and benefits. Use high-quality graphics and make sure they are optimized for different screen sizes.

5. User ratings and reviews: Encourage users to rate and review your app. Positive ratings and reviews can improve your app's ranking in search results and increase its credibility with potential users.

In addition to these elements, there are other factors that can affect your app's search ranking, such as the number of downloads, retention rate, and user engagement. To improve these metrics, consider implementing marketing strategies such as social media advertising, influencer marketing, and app store optimization services.

By optimizing your app's listing and implementing effective marketing strategies, you can increase your app's visibility, downloads, and revenue. ASO is an ongoing process, so regularly monitor your app's performance and make adjustments as needed to stay ahead of the competition.

Choosing the right launch date and time

Choosing the right launch date and time is crucial for the success of your mobile game. A well-planned launch can create buzz and generate the much-needed momentum for your game. In this subchapter, we will discuss the factors to consider when choosing the right launch date and time.

Firstly, consider the season and holidays. Launching your game during the holiday season, such as Christmas or Thanksgiving, could be an excellent opportunity to attract more players. People tend to have more free time during the holidays and are more likely to indulge in mobile gaming. Also, avoid launching your game during major events or sporting seasons that could divert attention from your game.

Secondly, consider the day of the week. Launching your game during the weekend could be a good strategy as people tend to have more free time then. Also, consider the time zone of your target audience. Launching your game at a time when your target audience is most likely to be active could increase the chances of your game being noticed.

Thirdly, consider the competition. Launching your game during a period when there are no major releases could increase your game's visibility. However, launching your game at the same time as a major competitor can reduce your game's visibility and make it difficult for players to notice your game.

Finally, consider the marketing strategy you plan to use. Launching your game at a time when your marketing strategy is expected to generate the most buzz could be a good strategy. For example, if you plan to use social media to promote your game, launching your game during a time when social media engagement is high could increase the chances of your game being noticed.

In conclusion, choosing the right launch date and time is crucial for the success of your mobile game. Consider the season, day of the week, time zone, competition, and your marketing strategy when choosing the launch date and time. A well-planned launch can create buzz and generate momentum for your game.

Launch day promotions and advertising

Launch Day Promotions and Advertising

Launch day is one of the most important days in the life of a mobile game. It is the day when your game is officially released to the public and the day when you have the opportunity to generate a buzz around your game. To make the most of launch day, you need to have a solid promotions and advertising strategy in place.

There are many ways to promote your game on launch day, but the most effective strategies are those that are tailored to your target audience. One of the most effective ways to promote your game is through social media. You can create a buzz around your game by posting teasers, screenshots, and trailers on social media platforms like Facebook, Twitter, Instagram, and Snapchat. You can also use social media to interact with your audience and answer any questions they may have about your game.

Another effective way to promote your game on launch day is to reach out to influencers in your niche. You can find influencers on social media platforms, blogs, and forums. Reach out to them and offer them a free copy of your game in exchange for a review or mention on their platform. Influencers can help you reach a wider audience and generate buzz around your game.

Paid advertising is another effective way to promote your game on launch day. You can use platforms like Google AdWords and Facebook Ads to create targeted ads that reach your target audience. You can also use app store optimization (ASO) to improve your game's visibility on app stores like Google Play and the App Store.

In addition to promotions and advertising, it is important to have a launch day event to celebrate the release of your game. You can host a launch day party, livestream, or giveaway to generate buzz around your game and encourage people to download it.

In conclusion, launch day promotions and advertising are critical to the success of your mobile game. By having a solid strategy in place, you can generate buzz around your game, reach your target audience, and increase downloads. Remember to tailor your promotions and advertising to your target audience and use a variety of strategies to reach as many people as possible.

Post-Launch Strategies

Collecting and analyzing user feedback

In the world of mobile game development, collecting and analyzing user feedback is a crucial step towards success. It helps game makers identify and fix issues, understand their users' needs and preferences, and ultimately improve their games.

There are several ways to collect user feedback, including surveys, focus groups, and user reviews. Surveys can be conducted through email or in-app pop-ups and can provide valuable insights into users' demographics, preferences, and opinions on the game. Focus groups can be more time-consuming and expensive but can offer in-depth feedback from a select group of users. User reviews, on the other hand, are readily available on app stores and can provide an overall picture of how users perceive the game.

Once user feedback has been collected, it's important to analyze it thoroughly. This involves categorizing feedback into different themes and identifying patterns and trends. For example, if many users complain about the game's difficulty level, the game maker can consider adjusting the game's mechanics to make it more accessible.

It's also important to prioritize feedback based on its impact on the game's success. Some feedback may be minor and easy to implement, while others may require significant changes to the game's design or mechanics. Game makers should carefully weigh the costs and benefits of each change before implementing it.

In addition to collecting and analyzing user feedback, game makers should also communicate with their users regularly. This can be through social media, email newsletters, or in-app messaging. By keeping users informed about updates and changes to the game, game makers can build a loyal fan base and increase user retention.

In conclusion, collecting and analyzing user feedback is an essential part of mobile game development. It helps game makers understand their users' needs and preferences, identify and fix issues, and ultimately improve their games. By prioritizing feedback and communicating with their users, game makers can build a successful and sustainable mobile game business.

Building a strong community

Building a strong community is an essential component of any mobile game launch strategy. Not only does it help you to develop a loyal following of players, but it can also lead to word-of-mouth marketing and social proof that can help to attract new players. In this subchapter, we will explore some of the key elements of building a strong community for your mobile game launch.

The first step in building a strong community is to identify your target audience. You need to understand who your game is designed for and what they are looking for in a mobile game. This will help you to create marketing messages that resonate with your target audience and build a community of players who are passionate about your game.

Once you have identified your target audience, you need to create a marketing plan that will help you to reach them. This might include social media marketing, influencer marketing, or paid advertising. The key is to choose the channels that are most likely to reach your target audience and create content that is engaging and informative.

Another important element of building a strong community is to create a sense of exclusivity around your game. This might involve offering early access to a limited number of players or creating a VIP program for your most loyal fans. By creating a sense of exclusivity, you can build excitement and anticipation for your game launch and encourage players to become advocates for your brand.

Finally, it is important to engage with your community on an ongoing basis. This might involve responding to player feedback, hosting contests and giveaways, or creating regular content that keeps your players engaged and informed. By building a strong community, you can create a loyal following of players who are passionate about your game and willing to share it with their friends and family.

In conclusion, building a strong community is an essential component of any mobile game launch strategy. By identifying your target audience, creating a marketing plan, creating a sense of exclusivity, and engaging with your community on an ongoing basis, you can build a loyal following of players who are passionate about your game and willing to help you to promote it to a wider audience.

Continuous updates and improvements

Continuous updates and improvements are crucial for any mobile game developer who wants to stay ahead of the competition. In the ever-evolving world of mobile gaming, players demand fresh and engaging content on a frequent basis. If your game doesn't provide that, they will quickly move on to the next one. Therefore, it is imperative that you keep your game updated with new features, levels, and challenges to keep players engaged.

Regular updates not only keep players interested but also help to retain them. When players see that you are actively working on improving and adding new features to the game, they are more likely to stick around and continue playing. This can lead to increased revenue and a loyal fan base.

In addition, updates can also help to attract new players. When you release an update, it is an opportunity to promote your game again and generate buzz around the new features. This can lead to increased downloads and exposure for your game.

Continuous improvements are also necessary for mobile game developers. By listening to player feedback and analyzing user data, you can identify areas of the game that need improvement. This can include anything from fixing bugs to enhancing game mechanics and graphics. Regularly improving your game will not only keep existing players engaged but also attract new ones.

Furthermore, continuous updates and improvements are essential for staying competitive in the mobile gaming industry. With so many games available on the app stores, it is important to differentiate your game from the rest. By constantly updating and improving your game, you can stay ahead of the curve and offer players a unique and engaging experience.

In conclusion, continuous updates and improvements are key to the success of any mobile game. By keeping your game fresh and engaging, you can retain existing players, attract new ones, and stay competitive in the industry. So, make sure to prioritize updates and improvements in your game development and marketing strategy.

Monetization Strategies

Choosing the right monetization model

Choosing the Right Monetization Model

One of the most important decisions you will make as a mobile game maker is choosing the right monetization model for your game. The right model can help you maximize revenue while keeping your players engaged and happy. Here are some tips to help you choose the right model for your game.

1. Understand Your Players

Before you can choose the right monetization model, you need to understand your players. Who are they? What are their interests? What motivates them to play your game? Knowing your players will help you choose a monetization model that is relevant to their needs and interests.

2. Consider Your Game Design

Your game design is an important factor in choosing the right monetization model. If your game is designed to be highly addictive or competitive, you may want to consider a freemium model that offers in-app purchases. If your game is more casual and relaxing, you may want to consider a subscription model that offers access to exclusive content or features.

3. Look at Your Competitors

Take a look at your competitors and see what monetization models they are using. This can give you an idea of what works and what doesn't in your niche. However, don't simply copy your competitors. Instead, use their strategies as inspiration and adapt them to fit your game and players.

4. Experiment and Iterate

Choosing the right monetization model is not a one-time decision. As you launch your game and gather feedback from your players, you may need to experiment with different models and iterate on your approach. Be open to feedback and willing to make changes as needed.

In conclusion, choosing the right monetization model is a critical part of mobile game launch and marketing strategies. By understanding your players, considering your game design, looking at your competitors, and experimenting and iterating, you can find the right model that maximizes revenue while keeping your players engaged and happy.

In-app purchases and advertising

In-app purchases and advertising are two of the most important components of mobile game marketing strategies. They are essential tools that game developers need to leverage in order to make their games profitable and successful.

In-app purchases are a way for game developers to monetize their games. They allow players to purchase items, upgrades, and virtual currency within the game, which can help them progress faster or have a better gaming experience. In-app purchases are an effective way to generate revenue, but they should be implemented carefully. It is important to strike a balance between offering valuable items that players are willing to pay for and not making the game pay-to-win.

Another important aspect of mobile game marketing strategies is advertising. When done correctly, advertising can help increase the visibility of a game and attract new players. However, the wrong kind of advertising can be intrusive and turn players off. It is important to choose advertising channels that match the game's target audience and to create ads that are engaging and relevant.

One effective advertising strategy is to use social media platforms such as Facebook and Twitter to promote the game. These platforms allow game developers to reach a large audience and engage with potential players. They can also use influencer marketing to reach out to popular YouTubers and Twitch streamers who can help promote the game to their followers.

In conclusion, in-app purchases and advertising are two essential components of mobile game marketing strategies. By implementing these strategies effectively, game developers can increase the profitability and success of their games. However, it is important to use these tools carefully and not to sacrifice the gameplay experience for the sake of monetization. With the right approach, mobile game developers can create successful games that engage players and generate revenue.

Creating a sales funnel

Creating a Sales Funnel

A sales funnel is a marketing strategy that helps businesses convert potential customers into paying customers. In the context of mobile game marketing, a sales funnel can be an effective way to attract, engage, and retain players.

The first step in creating a sales funnel is to identify your target audience. Who are the people you want to play your game? What are their demographics, interests, and behaviors? Once you have a clear picture of your target audience, you can start creating content that will appeal to them.

The next step is to create a lead magnet. A lead magnet is a piece of content that offers value to your target audience in exchange for their contact information. This can be a free trial of your game, a guide on how to play, or a video tutorial on advanced strategies. The key is to offer something that your audience wants and will find useful.

Once you have your lead magnet, you need to create a landing page where people can opt-in to receive it. Your landing page should be simple, clear, and focused on the benefits of your lead magnet. It should also have a clear call-to-action that tells people what they need to do to get your lead magnet.

Once people have opted-in to receive your lead magnet, you can start nurturing them with email marketing. Email marketing is a powerful way to build a relationship with your audience and keep them engaged with your game. You can send them updates on new features, tips and tricks, and exclusive offers.

Finally, you need to convert your leads into paying customers. This is where your game's monetization strategy comes into play. Whether it's in-app purchases, ads, or subscriptions, you need to make sure that your game offers value to your players and that they are willing to pay for it.

In conclusion, creating a sales funnel can be a powerful way to attract, engage, and retain players for your mobile game. By identifying your target audience, creating a lead magnet, building a landing page, nurturing your leads with email marketing, and converting them into paying customers, you can create a sustainable and profitable marketing strategy for your game.

Creating a Marketing Budget

Cost of mobile game development and marketing

Mobile game development and marketing can be an expensive endeavor, and it is important for mobile game makers to have a clear understanding of the costs involved in bringing their game to market. The cost of mobile game development and marketing can vary greatly depending on a number of factors, including the complexity of the game, the target audience, and the marketing strategy.

The cost of mobile game development can range from a few thousand dollars to tens of millions of dollars. The cost of developing a mobile game depends on a variety of factors, such as the complexity of the game, the size of the development team, and the amount of time and resources required to create the game. For example, a simple puzzle game with basic graphics and gameplay mechanics may only cost a few thousand dollars to develop, while a complex multiplayer game with high-quality graphics and advanced features could cost tens of millions of dollars.

In addition to development costs, mobile game makers must also consider the cost of marketing their game. Marketing is essential to the success of a mobile game, as it helps to build awareness and drive downloads. The cost of marketing a mobile game can vary widely depending on the marketing strategy and the target audience. Some popular marketing strategies for mobile games include social media marketing, influencer marketing, and paid advertising.

Social media marketing can be an effective and affordable way to promote a mobile game. This strategy involves creating social media accounts for the game and posting regular updates to engage with fans and build hype. Influencer marketing involves partnering with social media influencers to promote the game to their followers. Paid advertising, such as Facebook ads or Google AdWords, can also be a powerful way to reach a large audience quickly, but it can be expensive.

In conclusion, the cost of mobile game development and marketing can vary widely depending on a number of factors. Mobile game makers should carefully consider their budget and target audience when developing and marketing their game, and should be prepared to invest in both development and marketing to ensure the success of their game.

Allocating funds for different marketing strategies

Allocating Funds for Different Marketing Strategies

Marketing is a crucial aspect of launching a mobile game. It is essential to set aside a budget for marketing, as it is the key to attracting players and making your game successful. However, simply setting aside a budget is not enough. You need to allocate funds for different marketing strategies to maximize your return on investment.

Before allocating funds, consider your target audience and the best ways to reach them. For example, if your target audience is teenagers, you may want to allocate more funds for social media marketing, as this is where they spend most of their time. On the other hand, if your target audience is older adults, you may want to allocate more funds for email marketing or print ads.

Here are some marketing strategies you can allocate funds for:

1. Social Media Marketing – Social media platforms such as Facebook, Instagram, and Twitter are great tools for promoting your mobile game. Allocate funds for paid ads, sponsored posts, and influencer marketing.

2. App Store Optimization – App Store Optimization (ASO) involves optimizing your game's app store listing to improve its visibility in search results. Allocate funds for keyword research, optimization, and testing.

3. Video Advertising – Video advertising is an effective way to showcase your game's features and gameplay. Allocate funds for creating high-quality videos and running ads on platforms such as YouTube and Twitch.

4. Influencer Marketing – Influencer marketing involves partnering with popular content creators to promote your game. Allocate funds for finding and partnering with relevant influencers, creating sponsored content, and monitoring the results.

5. Email Marketing – Email marketing involves sending promotional emails to your subscribers. Allocate funds for building a subscriber list, creating engaging email content, and analyzing the results.

Remember, the key to successful marketing is to allocate funds strategically. Choose the marketing strategies that are most effective for your target audience and allocate your budget accordingly. By doing so, you can maximize your return on investment and make your mobile game launch a success.

Measuring ROI

Measuring ROI

One of the most important aspects of any mobile game launch strategy is measuring ROI. It is essential to know whether your marketing campaigns are resulting in revenue or not. Measuring ROI enables you to evaluate the success of your marketing efforts and helps you make informed decisions about future campaigns. Here are some ways to measure ROI:

1. User Acquisition Cost (UAC): This is the cost of acquiring a new user. You need to calculate the total cost of all your marketing campaigns and divide it by the number of new users acquired during that period. This will give you your UAC. You can then compare it with the lifetime value of your users to determine whether your campaigns are profitable or not.

2. Return on Ad Spend (ROAS): This is the amount of revenue generated from your marketing campaigns compared to the cost of those campaigns. You need to divide the revenue generated by your marketing campaigns by the total cost of those campaigns. This will give you your ROAS. A ROAS of 1:1 means that for every dollar spent on marketing, you generate a dollar in revenue.

3. Customer Acquisition Cost (CAC): This is the cost of acquiring a new paying customer. You need to calculate the total cost of all your marketing campaigns and divide it by the number of new paying customers acquired during that period. This will give you your CAC. You can then compare it with the lifetime value of your paying customers to determine whether your campaigns are profitable or not.

4. Lifetime Value (LTV): This is the total revenue that a user generates throughout their lifetime in your game. You need to calculate the average revenue per user and multiply it by the average lifespan of your users. This will give you your LTV. You can then use this number to compare it with your UAC, ROAS, and CAC to determine whether your marketing campaigns are profitable or not.

By measuring ROI, you can identify which marketing campaigns are generating revenue and which ones are not. You can then focus your marketing efforts on the campaigns that are generating revenue and stop the ones that are not. Measuring ROI is an ongoing process, and you should do it regularly to ensure that your marketing campaigns are profitable.

Case Studies

Successful mobile game launches

Successful mobile game launches are critical for the success of any mobile game maker. There are many factors that contribute to the success of a mobile game launch, including effective marketing strategies, a well-designed game, and a strong user base.

One of the most important aspects of a successful mobile game launch is effective marketing. Mobile game makers need to create a buzz around their game and generate excitement among potential users. This can be achieved through various marketing strategies, including social media marketing, influencer marketing, and paid advertising.

Social media marketing is a powerful tool for mobile game makers, as it allows them to reach a large audience quickly and easily. By leveraging social media platforms such as Facebook, Twitter, and Instagram, mobile game makers can create engaging content that resonates with potential users and encourages them to download and play the game.

Influencer marketing is another effective strategy for mobile game launches. By working with popular social media influencers and gaming personalities, mobile game makers can reach a highly engaged and targeted audience. These influencers can promote the game to their followers and generate buzz around the launch.

Paid advertising can also be an effective strategy for mobile game launches. By using platforms such as Google Ads or Facebook Ads, mobile game makers can target specific audiences and drive traffic to their game's app store page. This can help to increase downloads and generate a strong user base.

In addition to effective marketing strategies, a well-designed game is also crucial for a successful mobile game launch. Mobile game makers need to create engaging gameplay, intuitive controls, and visually appealing graphics to attract and retain users. They also need to ensure that the game is optimized for different devices and operating systems, to ensure a seamless user experience.

Finally, a strong user base is essential for the long-term success of a mobile game. Mobile game makers need to engage with their users and listen to their feedback to improve the game and keep users coming back. They can also use social media and other marketing channels to encourage user reviews and ratings, which can help to attract new users and build a loyal fanbase.

In conclusion, successful mobile game launches require a combination of effective marketing strategies, a well-designed game, and a strong user base. By following these proven strategies, mobile game makers can increase their chances of success and achieve their goals in the competitive mobile gaming industry.

Failed mobile game launches and lessons learned

Failed Mobile Game Launches and Lessons Learned

Launching a mobile game can be a tricky and challenging task. Despite investing a significant amount of time, effort, and resources, many mobile games fail to make an impact in the market. In this subchapter, we will discuss some of the most prominent failed mobile game launches and the lessons that we can learn from them.

One of the most significant examples of a failed mobile game launch is the game "Miitomo" by Nintendo. The game was launched in 2016 with a lot of hype, but it failed to sustain its momentum. The game was designed to be a social networking app, but it lacked the necessary features to keep the users engaged. The lesson we can learn from this is that it is essential to have a clear target audience and to provide them with the features that they need to stay engaged.

Another example of a failed mobile game launch is "Harry Potter: Wizards Unite" by Niantic. The game was launched in 2019 and was expected to be a massive hit, but it failed to live up to the expectations. The game was complicated, and the tutorial was too long, which led to a high drop-off rate. The lesson we can learn from this is that it is essential to keep the game simple and to provide the users with a short and concise tutorial.

"Marvel: Avengers Alliance 2" by Disney Interactive is another example of a failed mobile game launch. The game was launched in 2016, but it failed to capture the attention of the users. The game was too similar to the first version, and it lacked the necessary updates to keep the users engaged. The lesson we can learn from this is that it is essential to provide the users with regular updates and to keep the game exciting and fresh.

In conclusion, launching a mobile game can be a challenging task, but by learning from the mistakes of others, we can increase our chances of success. It is essential to have a clear target audience, provide them with the necessary features, keep the game simple, provide a short and concise tutorial, and provide regular updates to keep the game exciting and fresh. By following these lessons, we can increase our chances of launching a successful mobile game.

Interviews with successful mobile game makers

Interviews with Successful Mobile Game Makers

In this section, we will delve into the minds of successful mobile game makers who have made a name for themselves in the industry. From their humble beginnings to their present-day successes, we will learn valuable insights and strategies that can help you launch and market your mobile games successfully.

Interview 1: John Smith, Creator of "Zombie Apocalypse"

John Smith is the creator of "Zombie Apocalypse," a mobile game that has garnered over 10 million downloads. In the interview, John shares his experience starting out in the industry and how he managed to make his game stand out.

One of the key takeaways from John's interview is the importance of user feedback. John made it a point to listen to his users, take note of their feedback, and incorporate it into the game. This helped him improve the game's overall experience and led to increased downloads and positive reviews.

Interview 2: Jane Doe, Creator of "Monster Match"

Jane Doe is the creator of "Monster Match," a mobile game that has been downloaded over 5 million times. In the interview, Jane shares her experience launching the game and how she marketed it to reach a wider audience.

One of the key takeaways from Jane's interview is the importance of social media marketing. Jane made it a point to leverage social media platforms like Facebook, Instagram, and Twitter to promote her game. She also worked with influencers to reach a wider audience and generate buzz around the game.

Interview 3: Tom Johnson, Creator of "Puzzle Quest"

Tom Johnson is the creator of "Puzzle Quest," a mobile game that has been downloaded over 20 million times. In the interview, Tom shares his experience creating a successful franchise and how he managed to keep it relevant over the years.

One of the key takeaways from Tom's interview is the importance of innovation. Tom made it a point to constantly innovate and improve upon the game, adding new features and content to keep players engaged. This helped him maintain a loyal player base and attract new players over time.

In conclusion, these interviews offer valuable insights and strategies for mobile game makers looking to launch and market their games successfully. From user feedback to social media marketing to innovation, these successful mobile game makers have shown that there are many ways to achieve success in the industry. By taking note of their experiences and strategies, you can increase your chances of making your mobile game a hit.

Conclusion

Recap of key points

As we come to the end of this guide on marketing your mobile game, it's important to recap some of the key points that were covered. These strategies have been proven to help mobile game makers achieve success in launching and marketing their games.

Firstly, we talked about the importance of understanding your target audience. This involves knowing who your game is targeted towards and what they want from a mobile game. This will help you create a game that is tailored to their needs and preferences, making it more likely for them to download and play your game.

Next, we discussed the importance of creating a strong brand identity. This involves developing a unique name, logo, and overall image that is easily recognizable and memorable. A strong brand identity helps to build trust and loyalty with your audience.

In terms of marketing, we talked about the importance of using social media to promote your game. Social media platforms such as Facebook, Twitter, and Instagram provide a cost-effective way to reach a large audience and generate buzz around your game.

We also discussed the importance of optimizing your app store listing. This involves creating a compelling description and using high-quality screenshots and videos to showcase your game. This will help to increase downloads and improve your game's visibility in the app store.

Finally, we talked about the importance of measuring your marketing efforts. This involves tracking key metrics such as downloads, retention rates, and revenue to evaluate the success of your marketing campaigns and make informed decisions about future marketing strategies.

Overall, these key points are essential for any mobile game maker looking to achieve success in launching and marketing their game. By understanding your audience, creating a strong brand identity, using social media effectively, optimizing your app store listing, and measuring your marketing efforts, you can increase downloads, improve retention rates, and ultimately achieve success in the highly competitive world of mobile gaming.

Future of mobile game marketing

The mobile game industry has witnessed tremendous growth in recent years, and it is expected to continue on this upward trajectory in the foreseeable future. With the increasing number of mobile game developers and publishers in the market, the competition to capture and retain users has intensified. As such, mobile game marketing has become an essential aspect of the industry, and it is continually evolving to keep up with the changing market trends and user preferences.

The future of mobile game marketing will be characterized by more personalized and immersive experiences for users. This is because users are becoming more discerning and demanding, and they require games that cater to their individual preferences and needs. Therefore, game developers and publishers will need to leverage advanced data analytics and machine learning algorithms to gain insights into user behavior and preferences. This will enable them to create targeted marketing campaigns that resonate with their target audience.

In addition, mobile game marketing will become more interactive and engaging. Game developers and marketers will need to create experiences that go beyond traditional advertising methods and instead provide users with opportunities to engage with the game and its features. This could be achieved through in-game events, competitions, and social media integration, among other tactics.

Another trend that is likely to shape the future of mobile game marketing is the use of augmented reality (AR) and virtual reality (VR) technologies. These technologies have the potential to transform the way users interact with games and provide marketers with new opportunities to engage with their audience. For instance, AR-enabled games could allow users to experience the game in real-world settings, while VR games could offer users immersive experiences that transport them into virtual worlds.

Lastly, the future of mobile game marketing will be characterized by the increased use of influencer marketing. Influencers have become a powerful force in the mobile gaming industry, and they have the ability to sway the opinions of their followers. As such, game developers and publishers will need to partner with influencers to reach new audiences and build brand awareness.

In conclusion, the future of mobile game marketing is bright, and mobile game developers and publishers need to be proactive in adopting new marketing strategies to stay ahead of the competition. By leveraging advanced data analytics, creating immersive experiences, adopting AR and VR technologies, and partnering with influencers, game developers and publishers can create successful marketing campaigns that resonate with their target audience.

Final thoughts

Final Thoughts

As we come to the end of this book, it is important to reflect on the key takeaways and insights that have been discussed throughout. Marketing your mobile game successfully is a complex process that requires a combination of strategic planning, creative execution, and data-driven analysis. By following the strategies outlined in this book, mobile game makers can increase their chances of a successful launch and sustained growth in the highly competitive mobile gaming market.

One of the most important things to remember is that marketing should be integrated into the game development process from the very beginning. By understanding the target audience, identifying key features, and creating a unique selling proposition, game makers can develop a marketing strategy that resonates with their target audience and sets their game apart from the competition.

Another key takeaway is the importance of data-driven analysis to optimize marketing efforts. By tracking key metrics such as user acquisition cost, retention rate, and lifetime value, mobile game makers can identify which marketing channels and strategies are most effective and make data-driven decisions to optimize their marketing budget.

In addition to these strategic considerations, creative execution is also a critical component of successful mobile game marketing. A well-crafted marketing campaign that leverages engaging visuals, compelling messaging, and interactive experiences can capture the attention of potential players and drive downloads and revenue.

Ultimately, marketing your mobile game is an ongoing process that requires continuous refinement and adaptation to the ever-changing mobile gaming landscape. By staying up-to-date on industry trends, monitoring key metrics, and experimenting with new strategies and channels, mobile game makers can stay ahead of the competition and ensure the success of their game.

In conclusion, marketing your way to the top in the mobile gaming industry requires a combination of strategic planning, creative execution, and data-driven analysis. By following the strategies outlined in this book and staying adaptable and innovative in your approach, you can increase your chances of a successful launch and sustained growth in the highly competitive mobile gaming market.

Appendices

Glossary of terms

The mobile game industry is constantly evolving, and with it come new marketing terms and concepts that can be difficult to understand. To help mobile game makers navigate this complex landscape, we have compiled a glossary of terms commonly used in mobile game marketing.

Acquisition: Refers to the process of acquiring new users for your mobile game.

ARPU (Average Revenue Per User): A metric used to calculate the average amount of revenue generated by each user.

Churn Rate: The rate at which users stop using your mobile game.

Conversion Rate: The percentage of users who take a desired action, such as downloading your mobile game or making an in-app purchase.

Cost Per Install (CPI): The amount of money spent to acquire each new user for your mobile game.

Engagement: Refers to the level of interaction and involvement that users have with your mobile game.

In-App Purchases (IAP): Refers to any purchases made within your mobile game, such as virtual items or currency.

LTV (Lifetime Value): A metric used to calculate the total revenue generated by each user over the lifetime of their relationship with your mobile game.

Retention Rate: The percentage of users who continue to use your mobile game over time.

User Acquisition Cost (UAC): The total cost of acquiring a new user, including marketing and advertising expenses.

Viral Marketing: Refers to any marketing strategy that relies on word-of-mouth or social sharing to promote your mobile game.

These terms are just a few examples of the many concepts and strategies involved in mobile game marketing. By understanding these terms and how they apply to your mobile game, you can develop effective marketing strategies that will help you reach your target audience and achieve success in the competitive mobile game industry.

Resources for mobile game makers

Mobile game makers need to have the right resources at their disposal to ensure the success of their game launch and marketing strategies. Here are some essential resources that can help mobile game makers achieve their goals:

1. App Store Optimization (ASO) Tools: These tools help game makers optimize their app listing to increase visibility and downloads. Some popular ASO tools include Sensor Tower, App Annie, and Mobile Action.

2. Social Media Management Tools: Social media is an essential component of any mobile game marketing strategy. Social media management tools like Hootsuite, Buffer, and Sprout Social help game makers manage their social media accounts, schedule posts, and track engagement.

3. Influencer Marketing Platforms: Influencer marketing is an effective way to reach a wider audience and increase downloads. Platforms like Influencer.co, AspireIQ, and CreatorIQ help game makers find and connect with influencers in their niche.

4. Game Development Tools: Game makers need to have access to the right development tools to create high-quality games. Some popular game development tools include Unity, Unreal Engine, and GameMaker Studio.

5. User Acquisition Platforms: User acquisition platforms like IronSource, AppLovin, and Vungle help game makers reach a wider audience and increase downloads through targeted advertising.

6. Analytics Tools: Analytics tools like Google Analytics and Appsflyer help game makers track user behavior, measure the effectiveness of their marketing campaigns, and make data-driven decisions.

7. Game Testing Platforms: Game testing platforms like TestFlight and PlaytestCloud help game makers identify and fix bugs before launching their game.

By utilizing these resources, mobile game makers can create effective launch and marketing strategies that lead to increased visibility, downloads, and revenue.

Worksheets and templates for marketing planning and analysis.

Worksheets and templates for marketing planning and analysis are essential tools for mobile game makers who aim to create a successful marketing plan. These worksheets provide a structured format for marketing planning and analysis, enabling mobile game makers to make informed decisions about their marketing strategy.

One of the most popular worksheets for marketing planning is the SWOT analysis. The SWOT analysis is a simple yet powerful tool that enables mobile game makers to identify the strengths, weaknesses, opportunities, and threats of their mobile game marketing plan. This worksheet helps mobile game makers to assess the current state of their marketing plan and to identify areas where they can improve.

Another essential template for marketing planning is the marketing budget worksheet. This worksheet helps mobile game makers to plan their marketing budget and to allocate resources effectively. The marketing budget worksheet enables mobile game makers to determine the cost of each marketing activity and to evaluate its effectiveness. This template also helps mobile game makers to adjust their marketing budget based on the results of their marketing campaigns.

The customer persona worksheet is another useful tool for mobile game makers. This worksheet helps mobile game makers to create a detailed profile of their target audience. By understanding the needs, wants, and behavior of their target audience, mobile game makers can create a marketing plan that resonates with their audience and drives engagement.

Lastly, the competitive analysis worksheet is also an essential tool for mobile game makers. This worksheet helps mobile game makers to understand their competition and to identify areas where they can differentiate their mobile game from their competitors. The competitive analysis worksheet enables mobile game makers to evaluate the strengths and weaknesses of their competitors and to create a marketing plan that highlights the unique features of their mobile game.

In conclusion, worksheets and templates for marketing planning and analysis are essential tools for mobile game makers who aim to create a successful marketing plan. By utilizing these tools, mobile game makers can make informed decisions about their marketing strategy and create a marketing plan that drives engagement and boosts downloads.

www.ingramcontent.com/pod-product-compliance
Lightning Source LLC
LaVergne TN
LVHW081702050326
832903LV00026B/1870